BiBLE BREAKS

ZAPPING BOREDOM, FRUSTRATION, & TOTAL DISINTEREST

BiBLe BRain BReaKS

ISBN 0-687-34148-5

Art by Megan Jeffery; copyright © 2004 Abingdon Press.

04 05 06 07 08 09 10 11 12 13 – 10 9 8 7 6 5 4 3 2 1

MANUFACTURED IN THE UNITED STATES OF AMERICA

ABOUT BRAIN BREAKS

I am a teacher. I work with children, youth, and adults.

I am a brain researcher. I am continually learning how to be a better teacher because of my brain research.

My passion is to help others to be better teachers. I know it can happen. It is happening all the time.

Teachers who care about *how* their students learn, in addition to *what* they learn, are constantly keeping up with new discoveries into the cognitive processes. You must be one of those caring teachers, or you would not be reading this book.

We know there are things to do and *not* to do to help the mind function optimally. We know, for instance, that the brain needs oxygen and water. Deprivation of either causes the mind to become sluggish.

We know the mind needs to be challenged and to seek patterns. We know the mind thrives on novelty and becomes bored with "same old, same old." We know the mind works better at encoding information if it has time to reflect. We know the mind absorbs information in chunks. We know the mind needs to take a break every now and then to recharge and get energized. We *know* all of these things. We don't always practice what we know.

This book is not designed as a treatise on brain research. (See *Our Spiritual Brain: Integrating Brain Research and Faith Development* for more information on the learning brain. See also the bibliography at the end of this book.) This book *is* designed as a pickup book to keep nearby when you sense that your students need a brain break. You can find the brain break that will fit your students' particular needs at the moment. Specific Scripture references have been given for most activities, but many activities can be adapted to fit almost any Bible story or Bible verse.

Why do your students need a brain break?

- They may be suffering from information overload and need a boost of oxygen-rich blood to help them focus.

- They may need a deep-breathing break to help focus.

- They may need a challenge to kick their minds into high gear.

- They may need a drink of water.

Whatever kind of brain break they need, you can find it in, or adapt it from, this little book.

I invite you into the wonderful world of brain research. It is the most exciting place to be to help your students at any age learn and grow to their greatest potential.

Blessings,
Barbara Bruce

TABLE OF CONTENTS

INTRODUCTION

This Is Your Brain

The human brain is an amazing organism. It is divided into two hemispheres—left controlling the right side of the body, right controlling the left side of the body. The hemispheres are connected by fibrous tissues called the corpus collosum, which allows information to pass from one hemisphere to the other.

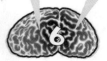

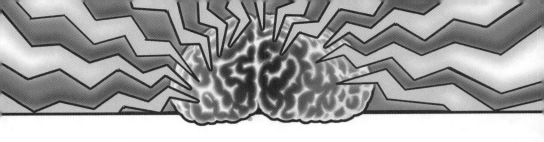

Historically, the left hemisphere deals more with concrete issues: words, numbers, order, and sequence. The right hemisphere deals with pictures, music, and creativity. For learning to be complete, you must engage both hemispheres of the brain.

The brain also has a quality known as "plasticity" that allows it to develop to meet the unique needs of each individual. No two brains develop in exactly the same way because no two people are the same.

What Your Brain Does and How It Does It

Your brain is superior at gathering and storing information. Each part of the brain has its own specialized learning tasks.

- The brain stem is primarily responsible for survival instincts. This is the part of the brain that kicks in and prevents learning whenever the person feels threatened, either physically, emotionally, or psychologically.

- The occipital (ok-SIP-i-tl) lobe of the brain processes the information that is gathered through vision.

- The parietal (puh RI i tul) lobe of the brain is where your higher sensory functions are controlled. This area receives direct outside input

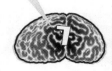

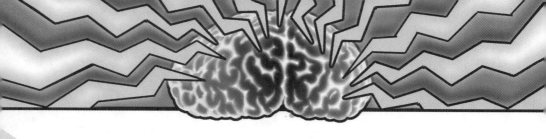

from your sense of touch, your sense of hearing, your sense of smell, and your vision.

- The temporal lobe of the brain processes the information gathered through hearing. It also controls memory and language.

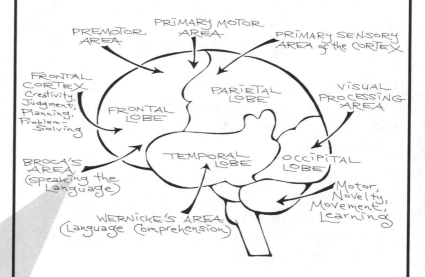

- The frontal lobe of the brain is the area where your logic, reasoning, judgment, planning, creativity, and problem solving are located. This lobe can only develop information provided by sensory and motor experiences.

A Little Bit About Neurons

What is a neuron and why is it important? Did you know that a fruit fly has 100,000 neurons, a mouse has five million, and a monkey has 10 billion? A human being, on the other hand, has about 100 billion neurons. (This information is from *Teaching With the Brain in Mind*, by Eric Jensen, © 1998 Association for Supervision and Curriculum Development.)

Neurons are essential to performing the brain's work. In fact, a neuron is constantly working. Its job is to pass along information. The more connections the neuron makes, the more information the neuron collects, the more efficient the brain becomes.

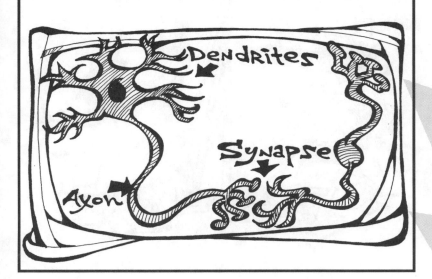

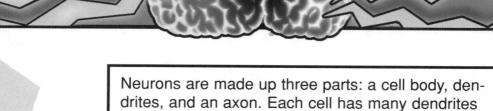

Neurons are made up three parts: a cell body, dendrites, and an axon. Each cell has many dendrites for collecting information, but only one axon for passing along that information.

A neuron's job is to take the information it is given and pass it on. This happens by connecting with other neurons. The more connections, the more efficiently the information passes through the brain.

The Theory Behind the Exercises

Have you ever felt like you were losing your students?

Do you ever notice signs of boredom, frustration, and total disinterest?

If you are among the zillions of teachers the world over who have experienced these departures from focused attention, there is hope! This particular brand of hope comes from the world of research into the learning brain. The most likely reason for students becoming bored and distracted is because their minds are not functioning at optimum levels.

What are Brain Breaks?

Brain breaks are exercises you can use for all age levels from young children to adults. The basic difference is the skill level involved and the amount of explaining necessary to introduce them. Use brain breaks when you sense that energy is dragging and your students need a boost. Use them when energy is "over the top" and needs to be refocused.

If you have been studying something for a period of time, both your brain and your body need a break to function at optimum levels.

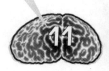

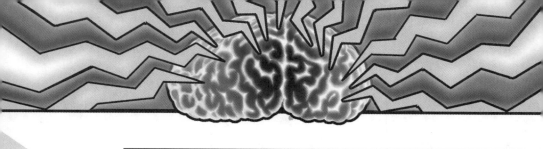

Think of a time when you have been in a class—you are paying attention, taking notes, and trying to integrate the new information. At a certain point your brain shuts down. You begin to zone out. Enough!

Wise teachers understand that this is *normal* brain behavior. The brain is sending a signal to the body—I need a break! It can be remedied fairly easily and with some interesting results.

When you stop what you are doing, take a brain break—stand, move, breathe, laugh, get a drink of water, and/or use your brain in a different way, several things are likely to happen:

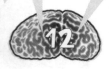

- You bring fresh oxygen to your brain with deep breathing.
- You challenge your mind to solve a quick and fun problem.
- You increase the opportunity to laugh, which has been called internal jogging.
- You work with attention span instead of fighting it.
- You move your muscles, which can become strained from holding one position.
- You hydrate your brain for optimal use.

How to Use This Book:

Most of the activities in this book will seem familiar to you. In fact, you've probably already used many of these with the students in your classes. Now you will know when to use them and why. The author has used these exercises in her training events with teachers and leaders in the church and with aging adults and care facilitators.

The book is divided in age-level categories— younger children (from 4–7), older children (from 7–11), preteen (from 11–13), and adult. Within each age-level category the brain breaks are divided into physical (those that primarily use the body) or mental (those that primarily use the mind). As in most experiences in life, there is some crossover. Often the differences lie in application rather than content.

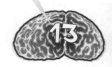

Because you are reading this book, you must have some interest in wanting to make your teaching/learning ministry more productive. Teaching in the church is a "soul making" thing to do. Treat this as a learning laboratory experiment. Follow a process and note the results. Make adjustments and try again. That's what teaching is all about.

Use the following process to experience the book:

1. Read through the complete book before you begin experimenting. Read all of the sections, not just those appropriate for your age level, so you can get a broader perspective and perhaps adapt or combine ideas for your age group.

2. Explain the theory to the boys and girls you will be working with. Tell them what you are doing and why you are doing it. You can usually tell when a brain break is needed. Once students are involved, and understand the concept, they can let you know when they need a break.

Bible Brain Breaks offers a win/win situation in that students' learning energy goes up, and they remember content at a measurably greater level.

3. Experiment. Try different kinds of brain breaks to discover which are more appropriate for your boys and girls.

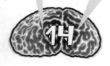

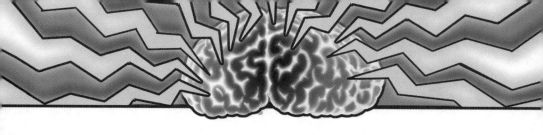

4. Check it out with your students. Ask for their feedback.

5. Experiment again and keep notes in the book of what works best. Adapt where you need to make it better for your group.

6. As you become accustomed to working with "brain breaks," you will get a feel for the kind of break you need. Some brain breaks add energy. Some involve connecting both hemispheres of the brain. Some generate oxygen. Some challenge the brain to solve a problem. Some are just fun. Remember, laughter is good for your brain. All brain breaks give the mind the break it requires to become focused again.

7. The format of the book is arranged by age groupings first. Then each section is divided into physical brain breaks (that involve the body) and mental brain breaks (that involve the mind). Both are equally necessary and equally satisfying to recharge and renew the brain to prepare it to focus again.

8. Within these two areas, the activities are broken down across broad age levels. Remember, not every brain break is appropriate for every class. As you are choosing, consider the maturity and temperament of children (and possibly youth or adults). Also take into consideration the age and ability of your students. This book offers you

choices. Some brain breaks will work better one day than another. It is the combination of your familiarity with the exercises, and your sense of what your students need that will guide your decision of which brain breaks to incorporate. The theory is sound. It is up to you, the practitioners, to test it for yourself and your students.

9. Try the exercises yourself before introducing them to your students.

10. Create a folder of papers to use at any time for bumper stickers, or create word searches or crossword puzzles at the beginning of each unit so you have them at your fingertips. You might find a computer whiz in your class who would love the challenge of creating these. (**Note:** This Web site may still be available to help you— www.puzzlemaker.com. You plug in the words and give them the guidelines for the difficulty of the puzzles. Then the site creates the puzzle.)

Remember, adding brain breaks to your lessons will be doing the brains of your students a huge learning favor.

Now, have fun!

16

PHYSICAL BRAIN BREAKS

Physical brain breaks are essentially of two kinds:
- Breaks that stimulate and energize.
- Breaks that quiet and focus.

Obviously, they meet different needs and are applied in different situations. Some of these brain breaks can be done with students standing next to their seats. Others will require a short "field trip" to another part of the room or even a hallway.

Some of these can be done in less than a minute (that's really all you need), while some take several minutes.

There is a rule of thumb that the attention span for younger children is about one minute per year of age. This can be expanded depending on the degree of importance and fascination. (My three-year-old grandson will play with his "Thomas the Tank Engine" set for about ten minutes, and then he is on to doing a puzzle or whatever strikes his fancy at the moment.)

The exact numbers are not that important. Simply understanding that the attention span of a young child is relatively short guides activities. Expecting

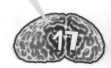

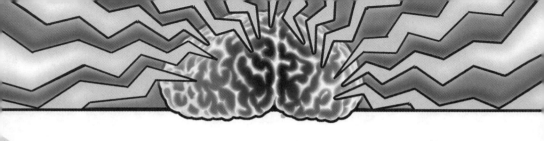

a young child to sit still and pay attention is a ticket for trouble.

Young children concentrate hard, and then they are off to something else. Their bodies are equipped with a natural brain break. Seldom do you need an energizing brain break with young children. Their brains are busy learning and experimenting with everything. With preschool children brain breaks can be programmed to help them focus.

WALK TO BETHLEHEM
BIBLE REFERENCE: LUKE 2:4-5

Setting up the Brain Break
Place a ten- to twelve-foot strip of duct tape on the floor in a straight line. Bring the children to the start of the strip.

Say: Mary and Joseph made a long trip to Bethlehem, the place where baby Jesus was born. Let's see if we can walk from Nazareth to Bethlehem too.

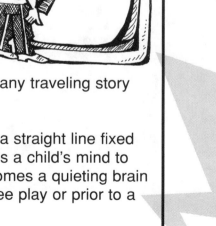

Brain Benefits
This activity will stimulate a child's sense of imagination, as well as help focus the brain. (This particular brain break can be adapted to any traveling story from the Bible.)

Inviting young children to walk a straight line fixed on the floor with duct tape helps a child's mind to focus. This kind of activity becomes a quieting brain break and can be used after free play or prior to a quiet activity.

Walking a straight line also helps the child to create and to maintain balance. Extending both arms aids balancing. Both hemispheres of the brain are required to work in tandem to complete this activity. The careful placement of one foot in front of the other aligns with the midline of the body and brain.

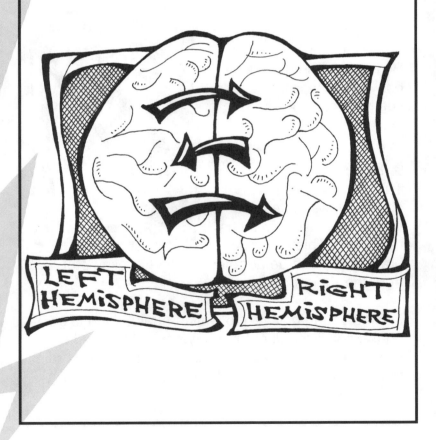

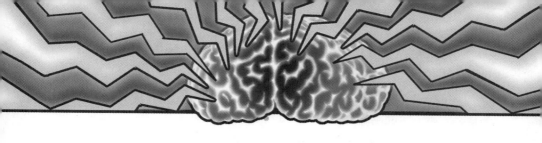

WALK FROM JERUSALEM TO JERICHO
BIBLE STORY: LUKE 10:25-37

Setting up the Brain Break
Lay out a random walking pattern on the floor of the room. Make sure there are no obstacles.

Say: Jesus told a story about a man who set out on a trip from Jerusalem to Jericho. Let's make the trip too.

Have the children place one foot in front of the other and walk along the random path you have created.

Brain Benefits
Walking along the pattern of a rope or duct tape laid out in a random pattern in a section of the room is helpful for intense focusing.

Use this as a quieting exercise to increase concentration. If you have access to a larger space, stretch the rope or tape to form a huge random design. This is a fun activity for children to practice balance and following a pattern in the guise of steps the traveler might have taken when he was beaten by robbers and helped by a man from Samaria.

WALK THE SHAPES AND SYMBOLS
BIBLE REFERENCE: GENESIS 9:12-13; MATTHEW 2:2; LUKE 23:33

Setting up the Brain Break
If you are working with Christian shapes or symbols, place rope or tape in the shape of the symbol you are learning about (for example, a star, a cross, a fish, or a rainbow).

Invite children to walk the shape, hop the shape, skip the shape, or crawl the shape. If your area is large enough, lay out several shapes. Let children select the shape they want to walk and report back to you what shape it was and why they chose it.

Invite the children to draw the shape or symbol they just walked.

Brain Benefits
For pre-school children crawling is a very helpful pre-reading exercise. This activity helps the mind to focus on right hand/left foot and vice versa. It also helps develop muscles needed to write and draw. If you expanded this activity to include drawing the shape, then you have also encouraged the mind to make the connection between the large muscle activity (walking) and the small muscle activity (drawing).

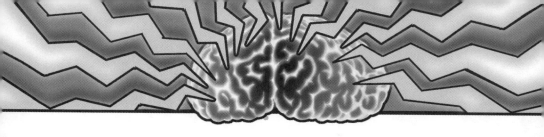

GOD'S LOVE IS INFINITE
BIBLE REFERENCE: MATTHEW 28:16-20

Setting up the Brain Break

Here is a wonderful and incredibly helpful brain break that focuses on Jesus' promise to be with us always, without end.

Say: Just before Jesus went to be with God, he told his disciples that he would be with them always, even to the end of the age. There is a symbol that we use to mean forever. We call this the *infinity symbol*. Infinite means that something goes on forever and never ends.

The infinity symbol looks like a number eight laying on its side.

Invite children to walk in a figure eight. Place two identical objects from your lesson (or pictures from your unit mounted on paper) on the floor about three feet apart. Have the children walk a figure eight around them.

Once walking the figure eight has been mastered, you can add other aids to cognitive functioning by:
• Swinging the arms opposite of the feet (left arm/right foot).

23

- Training the eyes to focus on a single object.
- Carrying on a conversation with another person while walking.
- Identifying pictures or objects.
- Reciting familiar poems, Bible stories, or Bible verses.

You will need to practice yourself and demonstrate several times until the children get it. Once they do, they will be walking, running, and skipping around the figure eight.

Brain Benefits

This technique is the concept of Dr. Deborah Sunbeck. The Infinity Walk has been tested and proven to increase brain function. By crossing the midline of your body, you fully engage both brain hemispheres. This technique was first used to help children with learning disabilities increase their cognitive functioning. The same concept can be used with all age levels and all ability levels. The Infinity Walk has even been used to improve cognitive functioning among adults who have suffered from strokes. For more information go to the Web at www.infinitywalk.com.

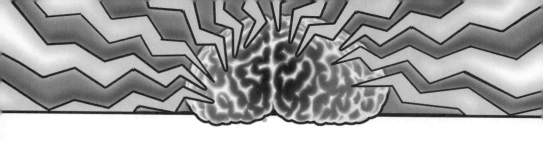

LOVE NEVER ENDS
BIBLE REFERENCE: 1 CORINTHIANS 13:4-8

Setting up the Brain Break
Say: In a letter Paul wrote to the church at Corinth, he told the people what love was like. One of the things he said was that love never ends, just like our infinity symbol.

Have the children create an infinity pattern by holding one thumb up at eye level directly in front of the body. With their eyes focused on their thumb, the children will move their thumb, creating a figure eight.

This exercise begins with the thumb at eye level, moving up to the right, down, over, and crossing the midline of the body, then moving down to the left and around, and back up to center.

The eyes follow the movement of the thumb at all times. When you have completed this exercise several times, switch thumbs and continue to follow the pattern. Practice this yourself several times so you can walk the children through the exercise.

Brain Benefits

This is one of the many exercises based on research done by Gail Denison and Paul E. Denison and recorded in their book titled *Brain Gym*. This resource is used by enlightened teachers across the country. Like the Infinity Walk, crossing the midline causes the children to engage both hemispheres of their brains.

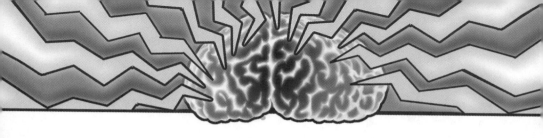

LEAPING FOR JOY
BIBLE REFERENCE: LUKE 6:23; ACTS 3:1-10

Setting up the Brain Break
Interestingly enough, sometimes an energy-filled brain break helps to *quiet* children down when they appear to be overly stimulated.

Ask: How do you think you would leap for joy?

If you notice children are too noisy, too busy, or too loud, invite them to stand and do ten leaps for joy as Jesus told us in the Sermon on the Mount or as the man whom Peter and John healed at the Temple.

Brain Benefits
This kind of controlled energy break diffuses the random energy, and children are ready to settle down.

MARCH AROUND JERICHO
BIBLE REFERENCE: JOSHUA 6:2-5

Setting up the Brain Break
Say: God told Joshua to march around the city walls of Jericho seven times. On the seventh time, the priests were to blow their trumpets. What do you think happened? The walls came tumbling down.

Invite the children to march in place for thirty seconds. Then tell them to raise their right hand when they march with their left leg, and raise their left hand when they march with their right leg. Have them take deep breaths as they march. Tell them they are like the Israelites marching around the walls of Jericho seven times until the walls fell down.

VARIATION: CLOCKWISE MARCHING
Invite children to march around the room clockwise once, then counter clockwise, as if they were marching around Jericho.

Brain Benefits
The lateral body movement (right hand, left leg; left hand, right leg) helps the brain to focus.

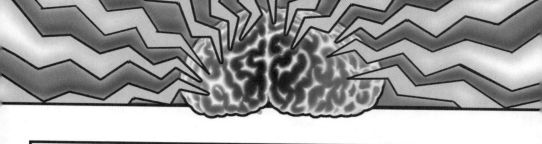

MIXED MOVEMENTS

BIBLE REFERENCES: MATTHEW 2:1-12; 14:22-32; MARK 4:35-41; LUKE 9:1-6

Setting up the Brain Break

Invite students to walk as if:

- They are walking in the Sea of Galilee.
- They are walking along a rock-strewn path through the mountains.
- They are walking on hot sand in the desert.
- They are walking in a windstorm on the Sea of Galilee.

This should give you some ideas to get you started. There are an infinite number of possibilities. Use your own ideas and coordinate them with the Bible story you are studying.

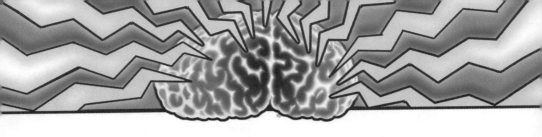

Brain Benefits

Not only have you engaged the child and focused his or her energy, but you have also called on each child's innate creativity.

MATTHEW MARK LUKE JOHN
BIBLE REFERENCES: FOUR GOSPELS

Setting up the Brain Break
Most children and teachers are familiar with the song "Head, Shoulders, Knees, and Toes." Instead of the familiar words, substitute the four Gospels: Matthew, Mark, Luke, and John. But use the same motions. Repeat. Try to say the names faster each time.

The first stanza will be:
Matthew, (*Touch head.*) Mark, (*Touch shoulders.*)
   Luke, (*Touch knees.*) and John, (*Touch toes.*)
Luke (*Touch knees.*) and John. (*Touch toes.*)
Matthew, (*Touch head.*) Mark, (*Touch shoulders.*)
   Luke, (*Touch knees.*) and John, (*Touch toes.*)
Luke (*Touch knees.*) and John. (*Touch toes.*)
Matthew, (*Touch head.*) Mark, (*Touch shoulders.*)
   Luke, (*Touch knees.*) and John, (*Touch toes.*)
Oh, Matthew, (*Touch head.*) Mark, (*Touch shoulders.*)
   Luke, (*Touch knees.*) and John, (*Touch toes.*)
Luke (*Touch knees.*) and John. (*Touch toes.*)

Brain Benefits
This activity helps diffuse excess energy and divert it into a manageable level. The movements encourage oxygen infusion into the brain. As a side benefit, the children will learn the names of the four Gospels.

Mental Brain Breaks

Mental brain breaks are designed to take your mind on a quick field trip to a different way of thinking. These brain breaks will challenge, stretch, and flex a child's thinking. You might want to think of these as mental aerobics.

As most teachers recognize, younger children learn as much with the bodies as with their minds. In fact, the more sensory experiences you can provide for a child, the better the learning experience will be. Separating physical and mental brain breaks is very difficult. But here are a few that will be fun to try.

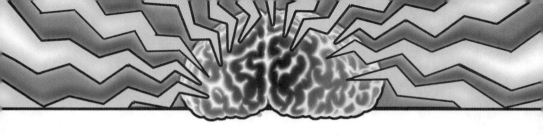

LEARN THE BOOKS OF THE TORAH
BIBLE REFERENCE: OLD TESTAMENT

Setting up the Brain Break
This exercise is a memory exercise done to a rhythmic or rap beat. The more familiar you are with the rhythm before you begin to teach the children, the easier it will be. Add rhythm instruments as the children become familiar with the pattern. Using these instruments also aids a child's memory.

Invite the children to sing to the beat as outlined below, clapping one time for each name, except for Deuteronomy. Break Deuteronomy up as shown below, clapping one time for each syllable. Practice several times.

Genesis (*Clap.*)
Exodus (*Clap.*)
Leviticus (*Clap.*)
Numbers (*Clap.*),
Deu (*Clap.*) te (*Clap.*) ron (*Clap.*) o (*Clap.*) my. (*Clap.*)

Brain Benefits
Any kind of pattern or rhythm stimulates the brain and makes learning easier. When you add instruments, you include more body movement and also increase learning.

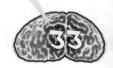

DRAW THE STORY
BIBLE REFERENCE: VARIOUS

Setting up the Brain Break
Select a character or scene from the story you are studying. Give children paper and pencils. Ask them to draw the character or scene with as much detail as possible. If it is a character, draw facial expressions, clothing, things they may be carrying, background, and so forth.

With practice this mental activity will encode details of the story in the minds of the children. (This activity works with people of all ages.)

Brain Benefits
Translating an image from the mind to a piece of paper is a multi-level learning experience. The activity goes from being primarily a verbal experience to a visual experience. Further increase the learning by allowing the children to explain their pictures.

SHARED STORYTELLING
BIBLE REFERENCE: VARIOUS

Setting up the Brain Break
Invite the children to find a partner. Have them sit in chairs or on the floor, facing each other.

Say: I want you to tell the story to each other. But you will do it in a special way. The first partner will tell one incident in the Bible story we just heard. Then the second partner will tell what happened next. Then the first partner will continue. Go back and forth until you have finished the story.

The children can help each other remember by prompting.

Brain Benefits
This retelling the story helps to imprint it on their minds.

35

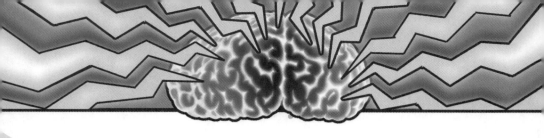

SENSING THE STORY
BIBLE REFERENCE: VARIOUS

Setting up the Brain Break
Scan the Bible story for sensory experiences that you can share with the boys and girls.

For example, in the Easter story you might include a jar of incense (room freshener), a stone, sand, a basket, and linen cloths. Allow the children to touch and/or smell the various items.

The birth narrative also works well. Provide several brown lunch bags. Put something from the birth narrative in each one—hay, wool, rough cloth for shepherds' cloaks, and a wooden board for the stable. Use your imagination. Invite children to tell the part of the story represented by what is in the bag simply by touching, smelling, shaking. Try these senses first, then let them look and retell the story.

Brain Benefits
Since we know that each of our senses is encoded in a different area of the brain, the more areas of the brain you include, the more complete the learning will be.

36

PHYSICAL BRAIN BREAKS

ENERGY SLOW DOWN
BIBLE REFERENCE: PSALM 37:7; 46:10

Setting up the Brain Break
Every teacher has experienced a time when the children have become over-energetic. A good way to slow them down is to change the pace slightly.

Turn the lights out, or gently blow a whistle to get their attention. Have the children sit down, put their hands on the table, and lay their heads on their hands.

Say: Be still, and know that I am God. Take three deep cleansing breaths. Now, breathe in for the count of three and out for the count of six.

This is not as easy as it sounds. It takes some discipline to manage the in-and-out pattern.

Brain Benefits
Not only does this exercise require concentration, but it also provides a good supply of oxygen to the brain and serves as a calming time.

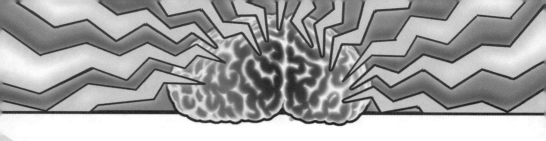

SYMBOLS, SYMBOLS, SYMBOLS
BIBLE REFERENCE: VARIOUS

Setting up the Brain Break
Say: Think of a symbol that you see in our church sanctuary. (*or a symbol in the Bible story you are learning about*)

If the children cannot think of any, suggest a fish, a heart, a cross, a dove, and a circle.

Then invite the boys and girls to select two markers or crayons of different colors. They will hold a marker in each hand. Give them a sheet of paper and have them draw the symbol on the paper with both hands.

Whatever the left hand does, the right hand must do the same. Allow twenty seconds. Then tell them they must cross over the midline of their body so the left hand is drawing on the right side of the paper and the right hand is drawing the same thing on the left side of the paper.

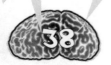

Note: This activity can also be done with paper taped to the wall.

Brain Benefits
The power of this activity is to activate both hemispheres of the brain in tandem.

CHRISTIAN STRETCHING
BIBLE REFERENCE: GENESIS 1:1-8

Setting up the Brain Break
If you want to activate sluggish children, invite them to stretch and breathe. Stretching and breathing moves muscles and increases the flow of oxygen to the brain. Stretching is also a wonderful brain break.

Invite children to stand. Have them reach down and touch the earth that God made. Hold this position for a count of three. Return to neutral. Then have the boys and girls reach up as far as they can to touch the heavens that God made. Remind them to keep their feet on the floor (no tiptoes). Hold this position for a count of three. Then return to neutral. Ask them to bend to the right to reach out to others they love. Hold this for a count of three. Then return to neutral. Repeat this on the left side, reaching out to those who are not loved.

Explain that it is important for them to breathe as deeply as they can and to reach as far and as hard as they can.

Brain Benefits
The increased deep breathing provides additional oxygen to the brain, which helps their brains to function at a more productive level.

SEEING THE GOOD IN OTHERS STRETCH
BIBLE REFERENCE: JOHN 15:12

Setting up the Brain Break
Say: In everything that Jesus taught, he told us to love others as he loves us. (*Have the children say the Bible verse: "Love one another as I have loved you."*) When you love other people, you recognize the good in them.

Invite children to stand with arms outstretched (not touching anyone else). Then have the children turn their head so they can look over their left shoulder as far as they can to see something good in everyone to the left and behind them. Slowly return to neutral (facing front). Then they are to turn their head to look over their right shoulder as far as they can to see the good in everyone to their right and behind them. Remind them to move slowly and breathe.

Remind the children to always treat their neck carefully and to stretch slowly.

Brain Benefits
This exercise crosses the midline of the body; it encourages stretching and teaches right and left.

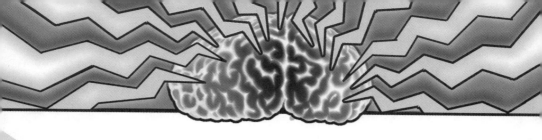

HUG YOURSELF
BIBLE REFERENCE: MATTHEW 22:39

Setting up the Brain Break
Say: When a lawyer asked Jesus, "Teacher, which commandment in the law is the greatest?", Jesus answered, "'You shall love the Lord your God with all your heart, and with all your soul, and with all your mind.' This is the greatest and first commandment. And a second is like it: 'You shall love your neighbor as yourself.'"

Invite children to give themselves a hug by wrapping their arms around themselves. Then have the children pat themselves on the back for a job well done.

Brain Benefits
This simple act is an affirmation. The brain responds well to affirming thoughts. These pleasant thoughts produce endorphins (natural body chemicals) that help the brain to de-stress. Remember, a brain under stress shuts down learning processes completely.

MENTAL BRAIN BREAKS

Mental brain breaks are designed to take your mind on a quick field trip to a different way of thinking. These brain breaks will challenge, stretch, and flex the child's thinking muscles. You might want to think of these as mental aerobics.

The mental brain breaks on the following pages are designed more for older children, those who are functional readers, ages 7–11.

The level of difficulty should, of course, be age appropriate and linked to the unit of study where possible.

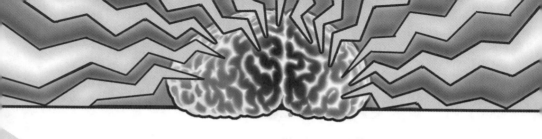

SCRIPTURE SENSORY STIMULATION
BIBLE REFERENCE: MATTHEW 4:18-22 (OR ANY STORY YOU ARE READING)

Setting up the Brain break

The latest brain research tells us that children remember best when they are involved with their whole body—this includes seeing, hearing, touching, tasting, and smelling. In order for the children to internalize the Bible messages they encounter, we must be willing to teach using all the senses. Each of the senses is wired to a different location in your brain.

Say: Stop what you are doing. Close your eyes. Think about the story we just read. Tell me about a color that you can see. Tell me about a sound you can hear. Tell me about a smell that is present there. What might you be able to reach out and touch?

For example, if you are doing the story of the calling of the fishermen, a color they might see could be the blue of the water, the golden color of the sand, or the brown of the wooden boat. A sound they might hear could be the waves, the sea gulls, the oars of the boat, or the wind. A smell they might encounter could be the fish, the ocean, or the sweaty bodies of the fishermen. A texture they

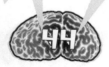

might feel might be the rough wood of the boat, the straw baskets, the rough rope and fishing net, or the scaly cool fish.

A harder one to visualize would be something they could taste. In the story of the fishermen, it might be the fish after they have been cooked, the cool sweet water, or the saltwater.

Brain Benefits
This activity forces the brain to concentrate on one area at a time.

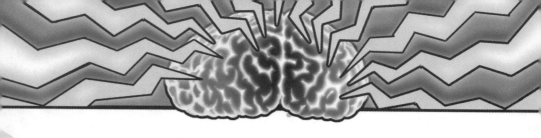

SCRIPTURE RIDDLES
BIBLE REFERENCE: JONAH 1—4

Setting up the Brain Break
Create your own riddles from the stories in your Sunday school unit. This simple activity helps children think in different ways and gets the brain on to a new thought pattern.

Here's an example of the kind of riddle to include: "What Bible-times character gave a fish terrible indigestion?" (*Jonah*)

A riddle break is fun and children can ask one another the riddles. If you plan for a box or bag of riddles, this becomes a quick pick-up-and-do exercise that works mental muscles.

Be certain that children can answer the riddles from the Scripture verses they have read.

Brain Benefits
Riddles and puzzles challenge a child's more complex thinking, which helps the brain to both focus and expand.

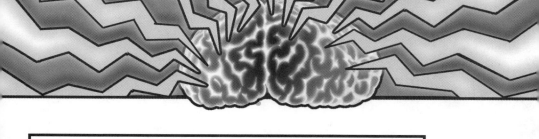

BIBLE-BASED WORD SEARCHES
BIBLE REFERENCE: VARIOUS

Setting up the Brain Break

Word searches are
easy to create. You
need a sheet of
paper with a series
of squares. First
print the familiar
words you want
from your unit of
study, using one let-
ter for each square.

With older children you can have up
to fifteen squares across and down.
Also, you can arrange the words in all
directions (forward, backward, diago-
nally, up and down). With younger
children, use only forward and up and down. Keep
the number of squares to ten. Then proceed to fill in
the other empty squares with letters at random.

Note: Print the words from the word search at the
bottom of the sheet so the children know which
words they are looking for. When creating your own,
make the word searches no larger than half a sheet
of paper so they can be a quick brain break.

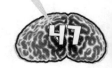

Brain Benefits

Word searches serve as brain breaks, because your brain looks for patterns. It will find words within the mixture of letters. Some curriculum units have word searches included in them. Use them as a brain break by switching the activity but not the content.

This activity encodes information from your unit in a fun way—the students learn by having fun.

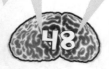

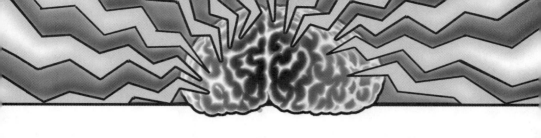

BIBLE-BASED CROSSWORD PUZZLES
BIBLE REFERENCE: VARIOUS

Setting up the Brain Break
Invest in a crossword puzzle software packet and create your own using familiar words from your unit of study. Either make these puzzles short, or allow only three minutes to see how many words the children can find in those three minutes.

If you create your own puzzles with words from your unit, you are reinforcing the learning while providing a break for your brain. Many curriculum units have crossword puzzles already created. The difference is how you use them. Tell your students they are engaging in a brain break by doing this puzzle.

Brain Benefits
This mental brain break gets the brain focused in a different direction so that it becomes recharged and will be more likely to refocus. The boys and girls will be creating new brain connections and sparking dendrites.

SCRAMBLED WORDS FROM SCRIPTURE
BIBLE REFERENCE: JOHN 3:16

Setting up the Brain Break
Create a sheet of paper with several words from a Bible verse in scrambled order. Invite children to write as many of the words correctly as they can in two minutes.

Level 1 (words in order, letters scrambled):

roF dGo os deovl het dorwl htta he veag sih ylon noS.

Level 2 (word order scrambled as well as letters being scrambled):

noS deovl roF htta het dGo ylon sih os dorwl eh veag.

Brain Benefits
Again, the brain seeks meaning and will make every attempt to identify the word.

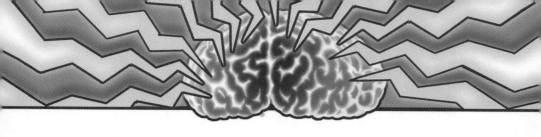

BACKWARDS THINKING
BIBLE REFERENCE: VARIOUS

Setting up the Brain Break

Ask the children to find a partner and stand face to face with them. The children are invited to tell part of the biblical story backwards, maintaining the integrity of the story. They must begin with the end of the story and work backwards. The partner keeps track of the accuracy. Then partners switch.

Brain Benefits

Having to think in reverse order causes the brain to focus in a different way. Anytime a pattern is changed and the brain is forced to re-activate, new learnings take place.

UPSIDE-DOWN BIBLE READING
BIBLE REFERENCE: VARIOUS

Setting up the Brain Break
Invite children to open their Bible to the Scripture being studied. Have them turn the Bible upside down. Then ask them to read the story (or verse) from this position.

This activity is fun, and students are amazed that they can do it. Obviously, you would not do this with children who are struggling to read right side up.

Brain Benefits
The brain is always seeking patterns. Changing the patterns and focusing the brain to learn in a different way re-energizes the brain.

PHYSICAL BRAIN BREAKS

Physical brain breaks are essentially of two kinds:
- Breaks that stimulate and energize.
- Breaks that quiet and focus.

Obviously, they meet different needs and are applied in different situations. Some of these brain breaks can be done with students standing next to their seats. Others will require a short "field trip" to another part of the room or even a hallway.

Some of these can be done in less than a minute (that's really all you need) while others take several minutes.

Preteens enjoy being silly and resist any activity that requires them to touch another person. Many of the activities that are included in the book for children can also be adapted for the preteen and youth audience. Brain breaks are especially useful for this age group. Oftentimes when a teacher perceives a "tweener" or youth as being bored, he or she is probably just tired. The preteen/youth body is growing and changing so rapidly, it is hard for their energy level to keep up. Brain breaks help restore the oxygen balance and reenergize them.

Be sure to use age-appropriate language and increase the challenge level. Some of the possible activities you might use that are included in the younger children's section are: God's Love Is Infinite (page 23), and Love Never Ends (page 25).

Depending on your group and their needs, adapt any of the physical brain breaks on the following pages. Remember to explain to your students why you are doing a brain break. Tell them that some of these activities can be done in their regular public school sessions before an exam to stimulate their brains to produce at optimum levels.

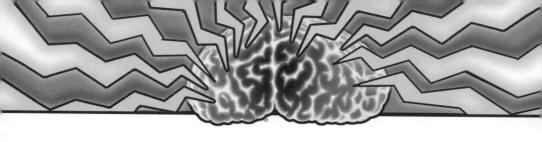

SCRIPTURE UNIT GROUP JUGGLE
BIBLE REFERENCE: VARIOUS

Setting up the Brain Break

Have several objects on hand. These Items might include a koosh ball, tennis ball, chalkboard eraser, keys, and so forth. Name each object for something or someone in your unit (James) as you hold it up. Invite students to form a circle. Tell them they are going to establish a pattern by throwing the selected named object to one another.

The rules are:
- Everyone must have a turn to catch and throw.
- They must throw to the same person each time to create a pattern.
- They must name the object (James) each time they catch it.
- The last person throws the ball to the person who began the exercise.

Ask if there are any questions. The object of this exercise is to create a pattern, not to make someone drop the object, so remind the boys and girls to throw carefully and gently.

Once they have established the pattern (practice two or three times), get the pattern started again.

When the first object (James) has been thrown to three people, start a second named object (John) following the same pattern. If they can handle it, throw in a third named object (Peter).

Brain Benefits

This brain break helps establish a pattern, focus attention, and create laughter (internal jogging). In addition, the extra movement will increase the oxygen flow to the brain.

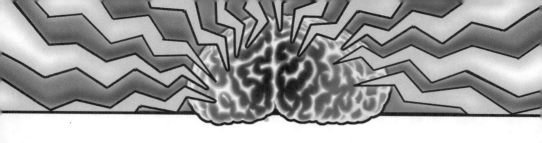

SYMBOLS, SYMBOLS, MORE SYMBOLS
BIBLE REFERENCE: VARIOUS

Setting up the Brain Break
Invite each student to lay a piece of paper flat on the desk in front of him or her.

Say: Select two markers (or crayons) of different colors. When I say "go," I want you to draw the same symbol with both hands. Whatever the left hand does, the right hand must do the same.

Allow twenty seconds—then tell them they must cross over the mid-line of their body so the left hand is drawing on the right side of the paper and the right hand is drawing the same thing on the left side of the paper. Some Christian symbols to consider are a fish, heart, cross, dove, and a circle.

Note: This activity can also be done with paper taped to the wall.

Brain Benefits
The power of this activity is to activate both hemispheres of the brain in tandem.

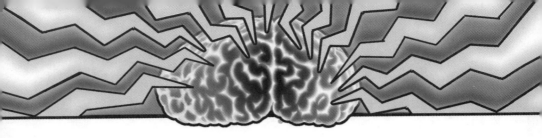

HAND-EYE COORDINATION AND SYMBOLS
BIBLE REFERENCE: VARIOUS

Setting up the Brain Break

Students can practice a hand-directed game. Ask for a volunteer to demonstrate with you while the children watch. Practice this particular brain break prior to teaching the children so that you won't have to refer to the book as you teach the movements. Explain that you will show them all the moves and then how to put them together to make a pattern.

Make fists with your hands. With your partner, gently tap the outside of your hands (little finger side) This action is called "CROSS." Then tap your palms (open hands) together. This action is called "HEART." Then tap the backs of your hands. This action is called "FISH."

Have the children select a partner. Have them practice the various signs: "CROSS" (tapping fists), "HEART" (tapping palms) and "FISH" (tapping backs of hands). Once students are familiar with the actions, ask for their attention again. Explain that there is a pattern they will follow.

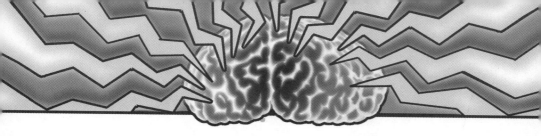

Demonstrate with your partner:

CROSS, CROSS (*Tap fists twice.*)
HEART (*Tap palms once.*)
CROSS, CROSS (*Tap fists twice.*)
FISH (*Tap back of hands once.*)

Invite students to practice.

Then demonstrate a more involved action pattern:

CROSS, CROSS (*Tap fists twice.*)
HEART (*Tap palms once.*)
CROSS, CROSS (*Tap fists twice.*)
FISH (*Tap back of hands once.*)
CROSS (*Tap fist once.*)
HEART (*Tap palms once.*)
CROSS (*Tap fist once.*)
FISH (*Tap back of hands once.*)
CROSS, CROSS (*Tap fists twice.*)
HEART (*Tap palms once.*)
FISH (*Tap back of hands once.*)

The rhythm and the movements will be picked up
quickly. It should sound like:

CROSS, CROSS, HEART,
CROSS, CROSS, FISH,
CROSS, HEART, CROSS, FISH,
CROSS, CROSS, HEART FISH.

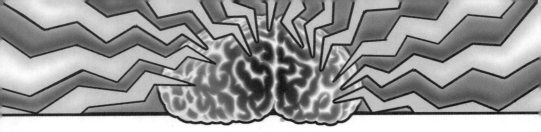

Note: I observed a kindergartner and a second-grader engage in this exercise for at least ten minutes on a train ride. When they made a mistake, they started over. They were training their brains to complete the pattern, following the movements by focusing their eyes and fully engaging in the activity. I have used this with youth and adults as well. Everyone has fun and is challenged—that is the point.

When students have accomplished this hand pattern, have them switch left and right palms with their partners. It is a game of concentration that takes only a few minutes to learn, but can take the brain to new levels of thinking.

When students have mastered this game and the hand switching, invite them to invent other movements and create a new rhythm.

Brain Benefits

This brain/body activity will spark dendrites. It reinforces learning and encoding in the mind. Remember, the brain loves patterns and seeks to make meaning of them. This is a great activity to refocus and reenergize.

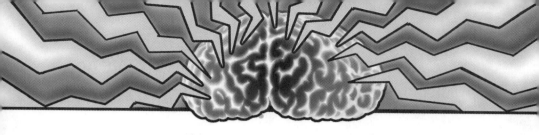

FISHERMAN'S NET KNOT
BIBLE REFERENCE: MATTHEW 4:18-22

Setting up the Brain Break
Say: The first disciples Jesus called were fishermen. Jesus called to them and they left their boats. Often the fishing nets became tangled. Part of the job at the end of a fishing trip was to roll the nets so that they would be ready for the next outing. Your brain break now is to attempt to untangle the fisherman's net.

Invite the boys and girls to form a circle. There must be an even number of people in the circle. Invite everyone to place his or her right hand into the circle and grasp the hand of someone across the circle. Then each child will do the same thing with his or her left hand, being sure not to take the same person's hand he or she already has. Everyone should have both hands connected to other people. Tell the students that their assignment is to become untangled. The only rule is they cannot let go of hands.

Brain Benefits
This exercise is physical, mental, and fun. If you have time to debrief it, you might learn many things about the leadership of your class.

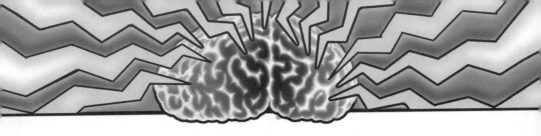

TAKE A STAND FOR CHRIST
BIBLE REFERENCE: Philippians 4:13

Setting up the Brain Break

Explain that *X*, which is the Greek Chi, stood for Christ over a thousand years before the English language even began to develop. Tell students they can take a stand for Christ by creating the letter *X* with their feet and arms.

Invite the boys and girls to stand with their feet together. Ask them to make an *X* by following these movements:

Step the right foot out and to the right, and then back to the center. Step the left foot out and to the left, and then back to the center. You have created a *V*. Now step the right foot back and to the right, and then back to the center. Step the left foot back and to the left, and then back to the center. Now you have created an *X*.

If this seems too easy, invite them to move their hands along with their feet: same hand/same foot. If this seems too easy, invite them to move their hands opposite of their feet.

Brain Benefits

Crossing the midline always forces the brain to engage both hemispheres. Using the arms and legs increases oxygen to the brain and reenergizes it.

GOD'S STEADFAST LOVE SURROUNDS ME
BIBLE REFERENCE: PSALM 13:5; 25:10; 26:3; 33:5

Setting up the Brain Break
Say: The object of this activity is to feel God's steadfast love within ourselves.

Have the students sit on the floor. Invite them to take a deep breath and let it out slowly. Ask them to sit with legs extended. Have them tense all the muscles in their body, beginning with their toes and working their way up to their face. As they are holding this tension, ask them to imagine God's love holding them tightly.

Hold this tension for five seconds. Then one at a time, have the children release their muscles. Begin with the toes, move to the calves, the thighs, the abdomen, the torso, the shoulders, the arms, the hands, the neck, and finally the face.

Brain Benefits
This isometric exercise of tightening and loosening muscles is good for complete focus and renewed energy. By incorporating the imagery of God's love embracing every part of them, each person can be affirmed as totally loved by God.

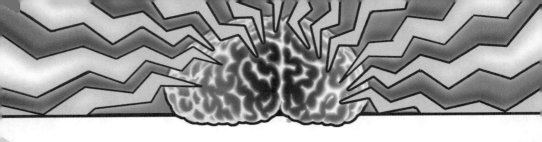

GOD'S LOVE IS INFINITE
BIBLE REFERENCE: MATTHEW 28:16-20

Setting up the Brain Break
This was used with the younger children, but is equally useful with older children (see page 23). Adapt the language to fit the needs of the children.

Brain Benefits
By crossing the midline of your body, you fully engage both brain hemispheres. The Infinity Walk has even been used to improve cognitive functioning among adults who have suffered from strokes. For more information go to the web at www.infinitywalk.com.

LOVE NEVER ENDS
BIBLE REFERENCE: 1 CORINTHIANS 13:4-8

Setting up the Brain Break
This activity was also used with the younger children (see page 25).

Brain Benefits
Like the Infinity Walk, crossing the midline causes the children to engage both hemispheres of their brain.

Mental Brain Breaks

Mental brain breaks are designed to take your mind on a quick field trip to a different way of thinking. These brain breaks will challenge, stretch, and flex the "'tweeners" and youth thinking.

The mental brain breaks on the following pages are designed more for youth (preteeners to 17). The same thing we said about the mental brain breaks for the other two age levels continues to apply here. Once again, the level of difficulty should be appropriate to the age level, and where possible linked to the unit of study.

Many preteeners and youth may think they are too old for some activities. But this doesn't mean you should eliminate all sensory activities. Simply change the language and the way you introduce each activity.

Mental Brain Breaks from the older children section that can be adapted include:

Scripture Sensory Stimulation (page 44), Scripture Riddles (page 46), Bible-Based Word Searches (page 47), Bible-Based Crossword Puzzles (page 49), Backwards Thinking (page 51), and Upside-Down Bible Reading (page 52).

BIBLICAL THEME SONGS
BIBLE REFERENCE: VARIOUS

Setting up the Brain Break
Break the students into groups of two to four persons. Give each group a list of biblical persons.

Ask them to come up with theme songs for as many of the following characters as they can in two minutes. For example, the theme song for Ruth might be "I Will Follow Him." The theme song for Noah might be "Raindrops Keep Falling on My Head."

Here are some suggested characters: Adam, Eve, Noah, Abraham, Sarah, Moses, Joseph (Jacob's son), Ruth, Samson, David, Esther, Mary, Joseph (Jesus' father), Judas, Mary and Martha, Jesus, and Paul.

Brain Benefits
Activities such as these force the brain to think in new and different paths. Anytime a new connection is made, learning becomes more efficient.

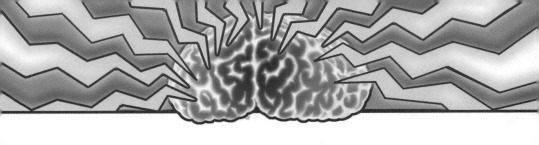

BiBle CHARACTER ABC'S
BiBle REFERENCE: VARiOUS

Setting up the Brain Break
Divide the class members into teams of two. Give each team a sheet of paper with the letters of the alphabet on it.

Say: You have three minutes to see if you can name a Bible character whose name begins with each letter of the alphabet.

Brain Benefits
This will be a quick change of pace and will re-energize the brain.

BIBLICAL PAIRS
BIBLE REFERENCE: VARIOUS

Setting up the Brain Break
This activity is particularly effective on the Sunday before Valentine's Day.

Say: What you have is a list of names. Each of these persons is one-half of a Bible-times couple. Can you name the other member of the couple?

Give each student a copy of the following names: Adam (Eve), Isaac (Rebekah), Jacob (Rachel), Samson (Delilah), Elkanah (Hannah), Joseph (Mary), Zechariah (Elizabeth), Aquila (Priscilla).

Brain Benefits
Recall and review of information that has already been learned provides stimulation for the brain.

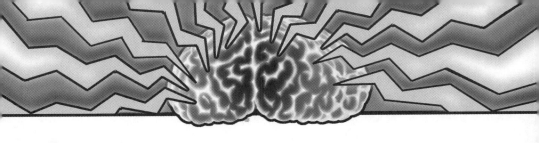

NEW WORDS FROM SCRIPTURE
BIBLE REFERENCE: JEREMIAH 1:4-5

Setting up the Brain Break
Take a long word from your unit of study and see how many words students can create out of that word in two minutes.

For example, if you were studying the prophet Jeremiah, you might use the word *prophet*. Here are some of the words that can be formed from the letters in the word *prophet*:

Prop, pet, top, hop, pore, tore, the, rope, hope, or

Use the names of the books of the Bible as a fun word activity as well.

Brain Benefits
Word games and puzzles create a challenge for the brain, which is always looking for recognizable patterns and ideas. Some persons thrive on this kind of learning.

69

CREATIVE FLUENCY
BIBLE REFERENCE: VARIOUS

Setting up the Brain Break
Produce an object from your lesson—the idea is to challenge the brain. Invite students to find a partner.

Explain that they will have two minutes to come up with as many uses for this object as possible. Anything works. Set a timer (or use a clock with a second hand) for two minutes.

Say "go." At the end of two minutes have students count up the number of uses for the object and report back. Some objects from Scripture lessons might be a water jug, seeds, coins, a towel, a shepherd's crook, and a piece of fishing net. The choices are limited only by the Scripture you are currently studying.

Brain Benefits
This activity forces the brain to go into previously uncharted territory. It stimulates creativity and causes the brain to re-energize.

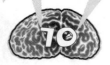

RiGHT HAND VS. LEFT HAND
BiBLE REFERENCE: JAMES 5:16

Setting up the Brain Break
Invite students to take out a piece of paper and write their name. Then challenge them to write it with their other hand.

Give the students a fairly short Scripture verse from your lesson, similar to the one referenced above. Have them write this verse with their nondominant hand.

Brain Benefits
This activity challenges the mind by making it direct the writing differently. To have the nondominant hand do something that is more frequently done by the dominant hand causes the brain to rewire. This increases the brain's fluency.

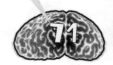

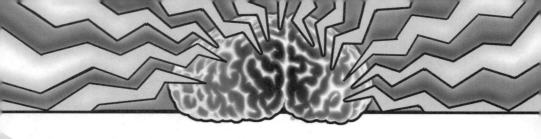

GIVE UNTO CAESAR

BIBLE REFERENCE: MATTHEW 22:15-22; MARK 12:14-17

Setting up the Brain Break

Say: Some Pharisees asked Jesus if it was right to pay taxes to the emperor.

Collect a penny from each student. Challenge students to recall everything that is on a penny.

Write the words *front* and *back* on a piece of paper. Allow ninety-seven seconds (use a timer or clock with a second hand) to record everything you can remember about what is on a penny. At the end of ninety seconds, hand the pennies back to the students and let them compare their answers with the real object.

Brain Benefits

This kind of mental exercise causes the mind to shift gears and focus in a different arena. At the end of this exercise, get a drink of water and get back on task, refreshed and ready to learn.

BODY OF CHRIST

BIBLE REFERENCE: 1 CORINTHIANS 12:14-21

Setting up the Brain Break

Say: In his first letter to the people of Corinth, Paul talks about many parts of the body all working together to make up the body of Christ.

Tell the students that just as the church is made of many people, the body is made of many parts. Invite students to come up with as many of the ten body parts that have three letters as they can in two minutes and fourteen seconds (eye, gum, ear, lip, jaw, arm, rib, hip, leg, toe). At the end of the time, ask for the lists students have come up with. Write the body parts on newsprint. Turn it over and ask them to recall the parts again without looking at their notes.

Say: This is a good place to teach *chunking*. Chunking is a quick way to help your mind remember things. The first five body parts are in your head (*eye, gum, ear, jaw, lip*). The second two are mid-body (*arm, rib*). The last three are in your legs (*hip, leg, toe*).

Brain Benefits

When you are trying to remember something, chunking it into smaller parts helps your mind remember.

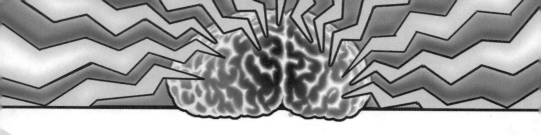

LIST OF TOP TEN THINGS
BiBle REFERENCE: VARIOUS

Setting up the Brain break
Most of the students are familiar with David Letterman's "Top Ten" lists. Give them an opportunity to create a few of their own. Here are several suggestions:

Top ten things you are doing to live the Ten Commandments. (Exodus 20:1-18)
Top ten things you are doing to prepare the way of the Lord. (Isaiah 40:3)
Top ten things you are doing to find time to pray. (Matthew 6:9-13)
Top ten things you are doing to love God with all of your heart, soul, and mind. (Matthew 22:37)
Top ten things you are doing to show friends you care. (Matthew 22:39)

Brain Benefits
This is a fun exercise that can have many variations. It stimulates dendrite growth.

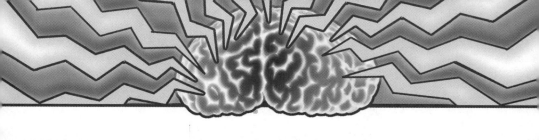

IF YOU COULD ASK GOD ONE QUESTION
BIBLE REFERENCE: EXODUS 20:1-2

Setting up the Brain Break
Say: Long ago in Bible times, many people had direct conversations with God. Adam and Eve spoke with God on a daily basis. Abraham and God talked about the land that God promised to the people. Moses acted as a go-between with God. If you could ask God one question, what would it be?

Brain Benefits
This stimulates creative thinking and sparks dendrite growth.

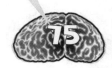

75

3:16 HUNT
BIBLE REFERENCE: VARIOUS

Setting up the Brain break

Invite students to open their Bibles and look up and mark as many 3:16 Scriptures as they can find in three minutes and four seconds. Mark them with slips of paper.

Invite some students to read theirs aloud.

Most people know John 3:16—arguably the most recognized Scripture around. But there are many other notable 3:16 Scriptures.

Brain Benefits

This stimulates creative thinking and sparks dendrite growth.

CREATE A SYMBOL
BIBLE REFERENCE: VARIOUS

Setting up the Brain Break
Most students can recognize symbols/icons of favorite fast-food restaurants, clothing manufacturers, and even singing groups.

Say: There are many different symbols we use in the church. We use the cross to remind us that Jesus was crucified on a cross. We use the star to remind us that the wise men followed a star to find the baby Jesus. The dove represents the coming of the Holy Spirit when Jesus was baptized. Symbols are usually simple pictures that represent more complicated ideas.

Invite the students to create a symbol/icon that states something about their faith.

Brain Benefits
Symbols represent a higher level of abstract thinking. When the brain connects a remotely related object to a more complex idea or event, then it creates a whole new system of neuron connections.

ANALOGIES
BIBLE REFERENCE: VARIOUS

Setting up the Brain Break
Provide a variety of objects from around the room. Invite students to select one. Their brain break is to come with a way that their object is like the lesson they are studying.

For example:
- How is masking tape (paper clip, marker, Bible) like the story of the Good Samaritan?
- How are scissors (rubber band, video tape, calendar) like the woman at the well?
- How is a box of crayons like the Creation story?

Brain Benefits
This activity forces the brain to think in different ways, which increases the connections between the dendrites. The more connections a brain has, the more efficient it becomes at learning.

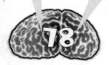

Physical Brain Breaks

Today's research on the brain and learning shows that there are significant links between movement and learning. We know this is true for children, but we also know that it is equally true for adults. Research has shown that not only does movement increase the oxygen flow to the brain, but it also stimulates the inner ear, which helps physical balance, motor coordination, and stabilization of images on the retina of the eye.

Most of the physical brain breaks for the preteen/youth can be adapted for adults. Depending on the age of some adults, however, be careful with a few of the activities. Also, keep in

mind that some adults do not like to participate in activities such as these. They think the activities are for children. They also may feel that they are too old to participate, or they are concerned about not wanting to appear foolish. Pick and choose your physical activities carefully with members of your specific group in mind.

Adults need brain breaks as much as anyone else. There may not be many adults willing to leap for joy in your room, but there are plenty of other activities you can try.

Adults will *usually* participate in these activities:

- Symbols, Symbols, Symbols (page 38).
- God's Love Is Infinite (page 23).
- Love Never Ends (page 25).
- Scripture Unit Group Juggle (page 55).
- Hand-Eye Coordination and Symbols (page 58).
- Take a Stand for Christ (page 62).
- God's Steadfast Love Surrounds Me (page 63).

In addition, try some of the brain breaks on the following pages.

MEASURED BREATHING
BIBLE REFERENCE: PSALM 46:10

Setting up the Brain Break

Invite students to take three deep and cleansing breaths. Now ask them to place their thumb and forefinger on their nose. They are to close off the right nostril and breath deeply in to the count of four in the left nostril only. They are then to close both nostrils and hold the oxygen in for the count of eight. They are then to open the right nostril and exhale to the count of eight.

This completed, they are to reverse the process, breathing deeply in with the right nostril only to the

count of four, closing both nostrils and holding the oxygen in to the count of eight and then slowly exhaling to the count of eight through the left nostril to complete one cycle. Tell them to do this complete cycle three times.

Brain Benefits

This breathing in oxygen, holding the breath, and exhaling slowly allows oxygen to enter the opposite hemisphere of the brain and remain there until it is slowly exhaled. This is a wonderful brain break to fill the brain with oxygen and to practice the discipline of slow breathing.

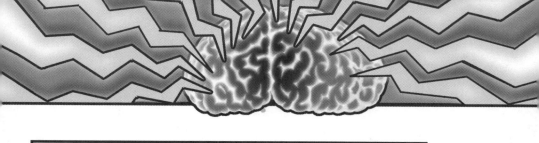

CREATE A LITURGICAL DANCE
BIBLE REFERENCE: PSALM 150

Setting up the Brain Break
Choose a hymn that is familiar to the group. Have them listen to the hymn all the way through one time. Then tell them to close their eyes and move to the music.

Say: Let the words dictate what the movements should be. Or you may simply let the spirit move you.

Variation:
Provide rhythm instruments, scarfs, or crepe paper streamers.

Brain Benefits
Movement increases the oxygen flow to the brain. It also stimulates balance and motor coordination.

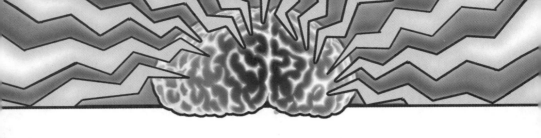

LEARN TO SIGN A BIBLE VERSE

BIBLE REFERENCE: PSALM 121:2

Setting up the Brain Break

American Sign Language is an excellent way to engage the body and the mind all at the same time. Use a particularly familiar Bible verse and teach the students the signs that are appropriate for the verse.

Shown here are the signs for the Bible verse: "My help comes from the LORD" (Psalm 121:2).

Brain Benefits

Incorporating movement into saying a Bible verse imprints the brain. It improves muscle coordination and increases the oxygen supply to the brain.

Mental Brain Breaks

Mental brain breaks are just as important for adults as they are for children. As a judge in Buffalo, New York, once said, "The brain cannot comprehend what the fanny cannot endure."

Many of the brain breaks used with children and preteens are adaptable for use with the older youth and adults.

Obviously, it is necessary to adjust the language and the content to match the subject matter you are studying. But try some of these:

- Analogies (page 78).
- Creative Fluency (page 70).
- Create a Symbol (page 77).
- If You Could Ask God One Question (page 75).
- 3:16 Hunt (page 76).
- Scripture Sensory Stimulation (page 44).
- Bible-Based Word Searches (page 47).
- Bible-Based Crossword Puzzles (page 49).
- New Words from Scripture (page 69).
- Backwards Thinking (page 51).
- Upside-Down Bible Reading (page 52).

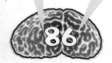

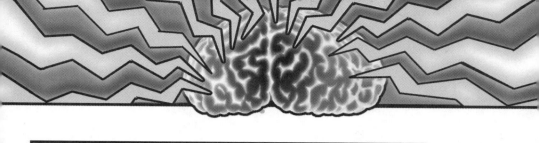

WATER, WATER, EVERYWHERE
BIBLE REFERENCE: VARIOUS

Setting up the Brain Break
Encourage the group to use their memory to come up with as many references to water in Scripture as they can recall.

Then get a drink! Encourage students to bring water, coffee, or tea with them and sip throughout the lesson.

Some possible Scripture references might be: Genesis 1:1-31 (Creation), Genesis 6:1–8:22 (Noah), Exodus 7:14-24 (water turned to blood), Exodus 14:1-31 (crossing the sea), Exodus 15:22–27 (bitter water made sweet), Exodus 17:1-7 (water from a rock), Joshua 3:1-17 (crossing the Jordan River), Jonah (Jonah 1–4), 1 Kings 17:1-7 (Elijah and the drought), Matthew 3:1-17 (Jesus' baptism), Luke 5:1-11 (calling the fishermen).

Brain Benefits
The brain is made up of 78 percent water. The body needs at least four to five glasses of water daily to feed the brain and help it to function properly.

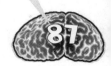

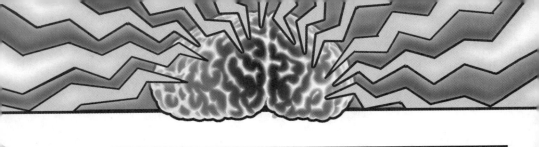

PUNCTUATION MARK
BIBLE REFERENCE: VARIOUS

?

Setting up the Brain Break
Say: Think of your faith as a punctuation mark. What would you be today? Why?

Make sure you give the students time to really consider this before asking for responses.

!

" "

Brain Benefits
This exercise forces your mind to take a different path. The brain constantly is seeking patterns, because this is the most efficient way to learn. Breaking the pattern is also good, since it puts the brain into a fresh learning mode.

.
.

*

,

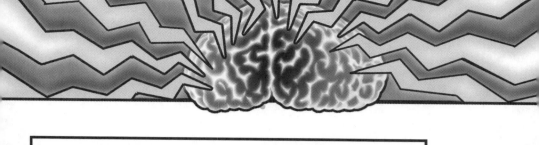

NOAH, METHUSELAH, AND YOU
BIBLE REFERENCE: VARIOUS

Setting Up the Brain Break
Have the students in your class think of at least five reasons they love their present age.

Brain Benefits
This exercise will make a person think in a positive way, which is always good for the mind.

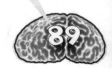

PAINTING SCRIPTURE WITH WORDS
BIBLE REFERENCE: MATTHEW 4:18-22

Setting up the Brain Break
Students will be in groups of six to eight. One person names an inanimate object or a person from the lesson. The person on the right adds a brief description of the object. The next person on the right adds more description, until all people have had an opportunity to add descriptions.

For example, in the story of the calling of the fishermen, a person might say: "Fisherman." The second person might say "Tall fisherman." The third person might say "Tall, muscular fisherman." The fourth person might say "Tall, muscular, long-haired fisherman."

If you have more than one group, encourage sharing the final picture with the total class.

Brain Benefits
Not only does this exercise promote creative thinking, but it is also a good memory boost.

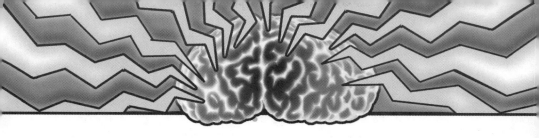

LET'S COOPERATE
BIBLE REFERENCE: GENESIS 1:1

Setting up the Brain Break

This activity will require a little more pre-planning. You will need index cards, two for each word of a particular Bible verse. On one set of the cards, write the words to the Bible verse. But mix them up. On a second set of cards write not the word but a clue for that particular word.

For example, in the Bible verse: In the beginning God created the heavens and the earth, a clue might be: "The third word in the Bible verse means the opposite of the word *ending.*" Obviously, the word is *beginning.*

Deal out the word cards to each person in the group. Deal out the clue cards to each person in the group. Then one at a time, let the persons read the clue cards and try to identify the word.

Brain Benefits

Not only does this activity promote cooperative learning, but it also stimulates the brain and helps it to refocus.

THE NUMBERS HAVE IT!

BIBLE REFERENCE: VARIOUS

Setting up the Brain Break

Say: Numbers play an important role in the Bible. I am going to give you a list of numbers, and you fill in the significance in the Bible:

Write the following numbers on a large piece of newsprint or on the board.

**1, 2, 3, 4, 5, 6, 7, 8, 9, 10, 11, 12,
21, 27, 30, 39, 40, 66,
100, 450, 3000, 5000**

Answers:
1: God.
2: animals on the ark, how Jesus sent the disciples out.
3: days Jesus was in the tomb.
4: Gospels.
5: stones that David chose, books in the Torah.
6: days people are to work.
7: days of Creation, time to forgive.
8: age when Josiah became king.
9: when the Holy Spirit came to the disciples at Pentecost.
10: number of plagues, commandments.

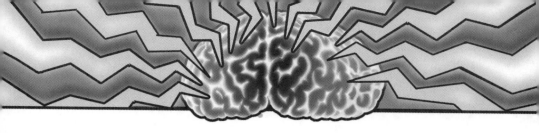

11: number of stars bowing down before Joseph in his dreams.

12: tribes of Israel, disciples.

21: letters in the New Testament.

27: books of the New Testament.

30: years of age when Jesus began his ministry.

39: books of the Old Testament.

40: years the Hebrew people wandered in the wilderness.

66: books of the Bible.

100: Abraham's age when Isaac was born to Sarah, number of sheep the shepherd had before losing one.

450: number of prophets of Baal whom Elijah challenged to call down fire.

3000: number of people who were baptized by Peter at Pentecost.

5000: men not counting women and children who were fed by the boy's lunch.

There are many more numbers in the Bible. If you like, use a concordance to expand your list.

Brain Benefits

This particular brain break will cause the students to think in a different way. It will refocus their energy and stimulate their thinking.

BIBLIOGRAPHY

Bruce, Barbara—Our Spiritual Brain: Integrating Brain Research and Faith Development; 2002 Abingdon Press.

Bruce, Barbara—Mental Aerobics: 75 Ways to Keep Your Brain Fit; 2003 Abingdon Press.

Denison, Gail, and Denison, Paul E.—Brain Gym: Simple Activities for Whole Brain Learning; 1992 Edu-Kinesthetics, Inc.

Jensen, Eric—Teaching With the Brain in Mind; 1998 Association for Supervision & Curriculum Development.

Michaud, Ellen, and Wild, Russell—Boost Your Brain Power: A Total Program to Strengthen and Expand Your Most Important Resource; 1997 MJF Books.

Howard, Pierce J.—The Owner's Manual for the Brain: Everyday Applications from Mind-Brain Research; 1994 National Book Network.

SCRIPTURE INDEX

SCRIPTURE   PAGE

SCRIPTURE   PAGE

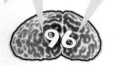